T0086247

Honor Among Thieves
(Poetry)

Peter Wuteh Vakunta

Langaa Research & Publishing CIG
Mankon, Bamenda

Publisher:
Langaa RPCIG
Langaa Research & Publishing Common Initiative Group
P.O. Box 902 Mankon
Bamenda
North West Region
Cameroon
Langaagrp@gmail.com
www.langaa-rpcig.net

Distributed in and outside N. America by African Books Collective
orders@africanbookscollective.com
www.africanbookscollective.com

ISBN-10: 9956-552-10-0

ISBN-13: 978-9956-552-10-8

Dedication

For all Ambazonian children orphaned by the ongoing civil war in Cameroon.

Foreword

Poetry has the potential to be therapeutic and cathartic, allowing poets to wade through existential conundrums in their lives; to find answers to nebulous questions of the moment; seek clarity in the midst of obscurantism; comfort and solace in malaise; peace and tranquility in a world gone haywire. Versification provides a vehicle for the exteriorization of diverse attitudes, frames of mind, and fresh insights. *Honor Among Thieves* accomplishes this feat. In this book of poems, the poet speaks in a confident tone of apocalyptic utterances: advising, warning, denouncing, protesting, and lamenting. This long poem has the twin virtues of relevance and clarity of diction. The poet willfully eschews the irksome ineloquence and syntactic sophistry characteristic of traditional poetry. He adopts the tone of African Guardians of the Word, the *griots*. Passion, energy, and incisive irony are the hallmarks of this didactic work. The poet subscribes to Salman Rushdie's conviction that "a poet's work is to name the unnamable, to point at frauds, start arguments, shape the world, and stop it going to sleep." In *Honor Among Thieves* music becomes a quest for the authentic self; songs serve as opium imbued with the power to transform weakness into strength, despair into hope. A bittersweet potion, *Honor Among Thieves* echoes the defiant voice of a son of the soil at odd with a world that has gone topsy-turvy.

"If you are offended it is your problem, and frankly lots of things offend lots of people."

(Salman Rushdie)

Basking in the solace/

Of mediocrity and myopia/

The 'People's Representatives'/

Metamorphosed nitwits/

Yap like hoodlums/

In the bowels of the Ngoa-Ekelle Glass House/

Handclapping semi-literates/

Kowtowing to the dictates of/

Diabolical machinations/

Orchestrated by an inept Executive/

Enchained by the wheeling and dealing/

Of foreign overlords/

Toying with the supreme law of the land/

Gerrymandering being the stock-in–trade /

Of self-styled band of demagogues/

These chameleons dance attendance/

On the threshold of the Etoudi Palace/

Macabre corridors of power/

To the chagrin of forgotten souls/

In the swamps of Elobi/

Of citizens chafing/

In makeshift shacks in Cassava Farms/

Hibernating in the dungeons of daily travails/

Ours is a tale of woes/

From Solomon- the-Tortoise/

Via Lawrence-the-Sheep/

To incumbent Djibril-the-Chameleon/

The rubber-stamping continues unabated/

Warthogs and toothless bulldogs/

Sparrow hawks and castrated peacocks/

Dance macabre in the putrefaction/

Of a throbbing heartbeat/

Suffocating in oversized strait-jackets/

Wherein they dare not budge/

Unable to see the limitations/

Of their own futile paradigms/

The possible advantages of an alternative/

Eludes these gawking-cum-fawning/

Accessories in heinous crimes/

Of national Auctioneering/

Intoxicated by the foams/

Of foul play/

Adept in the art of cooking-the-books/

A parliament of fowls/

Arms akimbo/

An emasculated Judiciary/

Pays lip service to the (mis)interpretation/

Of the letter and spirit of the law/

Trumped-up charges parade/

As bona-fide litigations/

Miscarriage of justice! /

Dereliction of duty! /

Harbinger of the dusk of Nationhood/

Weh! Weh! On va faire comment alors?[1] /

The voice of the voiceless /

Muted at gunpoint by home-bred Gestapo/

Joe La Conscience lays[2]/

Licking his wounds/

In the confines of Kondengui/

Altar of the rape of justice/

of the depersonalization/

Of prisoners of conscience/

The people poet/

Lapiro de Mbanga[3] alias/

Le Président des sauveteurs[4]/

The lone Voice of reason/

In a wilderness of irrationality/

Confined to solitude in the bowels/

Of home-grown Guantanamo/

Guantanamo left, right and center/

We've erected notorious dungeons/

All over the land/

Guantanamo at Tcholliré/

Our Nemesis!

History shall judge us harshly/

Very harshly indeed for our myriad/

Maximum security prisons/

How dare we be judge and

defendant at the same time?/

Guantanamo at Mantoun/

Held on perpetual lease/

Who controls this notorious hellhole/

4

Guantanamo at Kondengui—

Home to prisoners of conscience/

From all nooks and crannies/

Deprived of inalienable rights! /

Captives held in No Man's Land/

Guantanamo at the Douala Central Prison/

No access whatsoever/

to any form of legal counsel/

Sing requiem for Habeas Corpus! /[5]

Shame on the trumpeters of rule of law/

Shame on a nation that prides itself

on self-styled freedoms/

That's our Paradox!

Judicial aberration! /

Symbol of a legal limbo/

Mea Culpa! /[6]

Posterity shall judge you harshly/

harshly indeed for transforming/

this asteroid into a dungeon/

We beat them all/

Kirikiri/

Robben Island/

Guantanamo Bay

Et patati et patata./[7]

There's misuse of justice! /

There's reign of terror! /

There's murder of Habeas Corpus! /

Did I hear DEMO-CRAcY? /

Nay, me think it's DEMO-CRraZy! /

In these precincts/

Polls are seldom free and fair/

Hardly a litmus test/

for popular mandate/

Benefiting from the privilege/

of incumbency the powers-that-be/

make a sham of the ballot/

Ballot boxes filled with/

Counterfeit ballot papers prior to Voting day/

Ghost polling-stations set up/

In the palaces of Fons, Chiefs and Lamidos/

Private homes Metamorphosed/

into polling stations/

Sanctimonious hypocrites! /

Rassemblement Démagogique du Peuple Camerounais (RDPC)[8]

Electoral gerrymandering/

their stock-in-trade/

By foul or fair means! /

You're monsters! /

You tear people apart/

Your tongue is fiery/

Your lingo hate/

You call us *Anglofous*[9],

You brand us *Les Biafrais*[10]/

You think we're dirty *Mon Bamenda*/[11]

But who are you? /

You're the shame of humanity! /

Acme of human bigotry and folly/

Is there an identity crisis? /

I don't quite know who I am/

Je ne sais pas au juste qui je suis/

Some call me Anglo/

D'autres m'appellent Froggie/

I still don't know who I am/

Je ne sais toujours pas qui je suis/

My name c'est Le Bamenda/

My name is L'Ennemi dans la maison/

My name c'est le Biafrais/

Mon nom is underclass citizen/

My name c'est le maladroit/

Taisez-vous! Shut up! /

Don't bother me! /

Ne m'embêtez pas! /

Don't you know that je suis ici chez moi? /

Vous ignorez que I belong here? /

I shall fight to my dernier souffle/

to forge a real name pour moi-même/

You shall call me Anglofrog! /

Vous m'appellerez Franglo! /

Shut up! Taisez-vous! /

Don't bother me! /

Ne m'embêtez pas! /

Vous ignorez que I belong here? /

Don't you know que je suis ici chez moi? /

I shall fight to my last breath/

to forge a real lingo for myself/

I'll speak Français/

Je parlerai English/

Together we'll speak camfranglais/

C'est-à-dire qu'ensemble/

We'll speak le Camerounisme/

Because ici nous sommes tous chez nous/

A bon entendeur salut! /

He who has ears should hear! /

HEAR THE ANTHEM OF NATIONAL DISGRACE! /

National shame of prevarication…

DOUBLE SPEAK...

We're notorious for sugar-coated double-speak/

We make the ordinary seem extraordinary/

We employ convoluted lingo/

In a bid to veil our half-truths/

BIDON VIDES…

EMPTY VESSELS…

Faites confiance aux élus du peuple/

Have confidence in the elected leaders/

Vos routes seront goudronnées

d'ici peu dans les limites de nos moyens/

Your roads will soon be tarred/

If the resources are available/

Chose promise, chose due/

A promise is a debt/

Fiez-vous à vos élus/

Trust your elected representatives/

Tous nos hôpitaux seront

approvisionnés en médicaments/

dans les limites du possible.

All our hospitals will have/

all the necessary supplies/

if we can afford it/

Chose promise, chose due.

A promise is a debt/

Rassurez-vous/

Rest assured/

Tous les diplômés chômeurs/

seront embauchés aussitôt que possible/

dans les limites du possible/

all qualified job-seekers will be employed/

as soon as possible/

if we can afford it/

Chose promise, chose due/

A promise is a debt/

Soyez sûrs/

Tous les arriérés seront payés/

de tout de suit/

dans les limites de nos moyens/

Be assured/

All arrears will be paid at once/

if we can afford it/

Chose promise, chose due.

A promise is a debt/

Il n'y a aucun doute/

Toutes les écoles auront assez de/

fournitures bientôt/

dans les limites du possible/

There's no dobut/

All the schools will soon have enough supplies/

if we can afford it/

Chose promise, chose due/

A promise is a debt/

C'est certain/

Tous les retraités seront

Pris en charge sans plus de manières/

dans les limites de nos moyens/

Chose promise, chose due/

It's certain/

All retired persons will be paid their pension

Without further ado/

A promise is a debt/

Il va sans dire/

Tous les sans-abri seront logés/

sans plus de cérémonie/

Chose promise, chose due/

It goes with the saying/

All the homeless will be housed/

Without delay/

A promise is a debt/

Il faut toujours faire confiance/

aux élus du peuple.

You have to trust/

Your elected representatives at all times/

C'est pas du bidon tout ça! /

That's not all baloney! /

Caught in the throes of nostalgia/

For the 'good-old days'/

Midwife of an uneasy conscience/

Ours is an Animal Farm/

All animals are equal/

But some are more equal than others/[12]

Quips the sagacious George Orwell/

Ours is a cage of skewed minds/

Tortured by the pangs of uncertainty/

Of self-doubt and dreams aborted/

In the web of fate/

Ongola is stage where every/

Tom, Dick and Harry/

Comes to masquerade and make believe/

A podium for the showcase of moral degeneracy/

A forum where ethnocentric bigots/

Flaunt and fawn to the dictates/

of hierarchical de-constructionism/

A feeling of spiritual impotence/

Loams large when confronted with/

Barbaric acts of uncivilized scoundrels/

Vulgar oligarchic minions/

Inebriated by the blood of innocent corpses/

Fermenting in mass graves in Mbalmayo/

The hearth land of nihilism/

A stew-pot replete with/

cadavers of adversaries/

Jettisoned to rot/

In the Sanaga and Mungo rivers/

The ghost of Aya Kameni Patrick Lionel/

The phantom of Churchill Ambe/

Is up and about! /

Concoctions and potions galore/

In the horrendous pot-pourri/

Congruence of diverse impulses/

Divinities haunt us /

With telltale promises of vengeance/

Threats of impending/

Trepidation in reverential awe/

In outright defiance/

Of necromantic forces that stifle/

the angst of the downtrodden/

The land is rife with strife/

There's desire to wrench power/

From the bloody hands of political vampires/

Necks outstretched/

Mouths agape/

Teeth bared in readiness for mortal combat/

Street awash with the blood of /

Slaughtered unarmed citizens/

There's fire in the house/

RUN! RUN! RUN!

Traitors kiss the asses of ghost victims/

In mock atonement/

Clasped in the arms of the troika: /

Tribalism, cronyism, nepotism/

These are maggots/

Squirming at the fabric/

of an unimpressive edifice/

Shall they make or mar? /

Shall the populace absolve them/

From crimes committed against humanity? /

Shall we enthrone them in the guise/

Of latter day deities of/

Le Renouveau— the New Deal? /

The land sentenced to premature death/

It's time to lay the ghosts/

of divisive contraptions to rest/

And join hands in unison/

Together we'll see the world/

through a clearer prism/

It boggles the mind to fathom/

That we'll build this Nation/

by means of Divide and Conquer/

Modus operandi/

How can God continue to/

bless this vile Tribe of ours? /

Come to think of it/

our society has sent God to quarantine/

Schools are awash with drugs/

Kids tot guns with impunity/

Teenagers fornicate with no qualms/

Marriages are a sham/

Back-stabbing without precedence in the world/

Child trafficking and vandalism/

our stock-in-trade/

Religion transformed into/

a lethal tool for mutual annihilation/

This Tribe of ours is sick/

Very sick indeed/

God must be angry! /

We'll unite or perish/

It's time for fumigation/

Through the magic potion of action/

Man will free himself/

from the shackles of entrapment/

Through the action of Man/

He sets himself free from the cankers of inaction/

By means of action Man steps forth/

Makes quantum leaps/

In a bid to evade the Sisyphean humdrum/

Where each day resembles another/

Via action Man distinguishes/

Himself from other bipedal primates/

And becomes a full blown Individual/

Inaction compounds the complexities of life/

In a topsy-turvy of existence/

Marked by ontological ellipses/

We shall embrace action/

or privatize our legacies/

Don't privatize Mama Kamerun! /

Beware of matricide! /

Don't kill Mama Kamerun! /

Can you hear me now? /

Under her skin lies her beauty/

In her roots, her being, her soul/

Her essence, her skin/

With shades erratic/

Height ever so changing/

Her hair, curly, and long/

Straight, short and at times, like whatever/

Her worth measurable to none/

One Singular sensation/

She stands/Kind/

She is Loving, Beautiful and Generous/

Like Santa Claus/

With open arms she shares/

Her worldly worth and wealth/

To citizens and denizens alike/

And she is quite famous among material-mongers/

And faint acquaintances/

Blinded by false pretenses/

She blindly gives and gives/

And gives, and gives even more/

Allowing her soul and worth/

To be read and shared like an open book/

Selfish mongers endeavor to seize her entity/

Her home, her gifts, her land, HER PROPERTY! /

AND yet, her pride, her love, her joys

and happiness…remain intact/

She yearns for your embrace/

Attention! Screaming! /

Can you hear HER now? /

Alone as prey to pleasing others/

She forgot to please herself/

To Take care of herself/

And just B-R-E-A-T-H and B-R-E-A-T-H for once! /

Corrupted by infectious diseases/

War and hard times, her popularity collapsed/

Drowning like her presence was never existent/

From the sole in her step/

The beat in her heart/

She cries for help/

Reaching out her hand/

Hoping to find yours/

Your touch, to hold, and squeeze, to love/

To find yours to love/

To love and never to let go/

Just to know you are there/

She wants to feel love/

Like that of a mother to a child/

the nurture of her being/

Like best friends/

Who want to feel loved/

AND yet as it goes/

Alas! /

Where is OUR love for Mama Kamerun? /

We betrayed her/

We disowned her/

We brutalized her/

We raped her/

We choked her/

We despoiled her/

She screams… and wails melodically/

To tune of sorrow and need/

Her worries formulate an ocean of sorrow/

Crying you a river to know/

And feel OUR genuine presence/

So called friends flee/

False acquaintances/

Fair weather friends/

Running away from responsibility/

And loyalty to so-called essence/

of harmonious friendship/

They are no where to be found/

Still, her spirit, and energy/

Her pride, her love, her joys/

And happiness remain immeasurable/

Just to let you know… she is there/

MAMA KAMERUN!

Hear the cry of a bereft mother/

On her feet/

She breathes in and out/

In and out to feel love/

And air, and peace/

SHE BREATHES IN AND OUT TO FEEL LOVE/

AND AIR, AND…PEACE/

Then on her knees, she turns to HIM/

Her ultimate source of power and security/

And He gives her strength/

Yes He, gives her strength/

Then her Beauty shines/

like the sun, illuminating hope/

Her music and dance so seductive/

She could make a man sweat/

Her soul so tender, loves like thunder/

Sweet as honey, she could heal *Cameroonosomiasis*[13].

Because on the surface lies her enigma/

In her roots, her being, her soul/

Her essence/

And in her name, MAMA KAMERUN!

We've no choice but to march/

Steadily and inexorably toward/

A sounder knowledge of the demands/

Of nationhood and nation-building/

Obeying an instinct that obligates/

Us to work in tandem/

Benefiting from the errors of yesteryears/

A collective undercurrent prompts us/

To side-step despondency/

I see light at the end of the proverbial tunnel/

I hear the multiform cry of the disenchanted/

The lament of the rank and file/

Baying for an antidote to Aporia/

Locus of unbridled rejuvenation/

Power to the populace! /

Our folksong turned into a dirge/

Our liberation chant converted into a war song/

The Aborted Hallelujah of redemption/

Heed the vitriolic hymn/

Sung by Nooremac Mahatma Gandhi—Bate Besong/

Whose vituperations gave fainting feats/

To the powers-that-be/

Forget not Mongo Beti! /

National gadfly/

Whose penmanship is the cloth of our nakedness/

Let me mention Longuè Longuè/[14]

Alias Longkana Agno Simon/

Whose Hosanna of liberation is truer/

Than the spurious cacophony of the nation's/

Grave-digging chant— O Cameroon,

Thou Cradle of our Fathers…/Land of Promise, land of Glory! /

Ha! Ha! Ha!! / (laughter is therapeutic!)

Land of Promise, land of Glory, my eyeballs! /

The land is shaken to its very foundation/

By the credo of *Chop-broke-potism*/[15]

A battlefield for ego trade-off/

The malaise in the firmament/

Maybe due to the psychic residues/

Of an abscess awaiting deflation/

A state of affairs that spells collective doom/

Rigorous negation harboring seeds/

Of our own very antithesis/

Take a walk down memory lane/

And speak of a momentous "event"/

And let's use quotation marks/

To serve as a precaution/

What would that event be? /

The 1961 Foumban Plebiscite? /

The 1972 Peaceful Revolution? /

Or the 1982 Waterloo? /

The ouster of the most talkative zombie/

Haunts all and sundry/

The next EVENT will be the untimely exit/

Of a less garrulous scare-crow/

There'll be torch-light processions nationwide/

Not to mourn the passing of a Nonentity/

But to celebrate the end of Cancerous era/

The long-waited Panacea is nigh/

Neither prophet of doom/

Nor messenger of gloom/

Be it as it may/

Suffice it to say/

Dictators ride hither and thither/

On their paper tigers/

But dare not descend/

For fear of being devoured by demons of Karma/

There's no question/

This joint of ours is a stage/

where nincompoops come act/

Garbed in multifaceted masks/

folks make believe in all walks of life! /

Foes act like friends/

Friends mistaken for foes/

Mortals impersonate immortals/

Humans pass for prima donnas/

Miscreants act the pious/

Self-seekers masquerade as /

selfless philanthropists/

Servants of Satan spot the mask/

of men of God! /

Truth is this *pays*[16] is replete with impostors/

How long shall we dress in borrowed robes? /

How long shall we pull the wool/

over the eyes of folks? /

How long shall we wear masks? /

There's counterfeiting in the house…

Fraudster! /

Custodian of bogus certificates/

You, bachelier[17] of Bonamoussadi/

How do you feel in the

borrowed academic robes you wear? /

Certificates manufactured at Bonamoussadi /

Hey, *licencié*[18] of Bonamoussadi!

How do you feel brandishing a degree/

You did not earn? /

You've thrown pride to the dogs/

And rendered yourself

prisoner of your own conscience/

Hullo, owner of a fake *doctorat d'état*/[19]

Shame of academia/

Academic impostor!

Bow your head in shame/

Hang your neck in disgrace/

Because your deeds are no longer a secret/

Academic philanderer!

You trade sex for marks/

Do you feel at ease in your/

Sexually transmitted diplomas? /

Your school is the shopping mall/

Where you haggle over sex and grades/

Down with pseudo-intellectuals! /

Away with *kokobioko*[20] professors! /

To Hades with *Kabukabu*[21] scholars! /

Liberate yourselves from mental slavery/

Free yourselves from self-imposed incarceration/

Dispose of all ill-gotten qualifications/

And begin from scratch/

Throw off your manacles/

That is purgative! /

We're in chains! /

If wishes were horses/

beggars would ride/

Alas, life's seldom a free ride/

You can't eat your cake and have it/

Beggars can't be choosers/

Man is born free but in chains everywhere/

Fetters of daily toil/

Chains of substance abuse/

shackles of social upheavals/

Chains of moral decadence/

Manacles of infidelity/

Chains of cerebral servitude/

Bonds of fundamentalist bigotry/

Chains of imperialist yoke/

Away with shackles of bondage!/

Mankind is hard at work decimating womenfolk/

We build castles in the air/

Womankind is engrossed/

in the unholy task of undoing mankind!/

Each passing day portends woe/

for humanity's fateful predicament/

Takes a third eye to see what I see/

Watch yourself go by day in day out/

Perceive yourself as "He", not "I." /

Find fault with yourself as you'd with others/

Confront yourself unabashedly/

Watch yourself go by each day/

Read meaning into your every intention/

in the same manner you would judge others/

Let unmitigated criticism surge through you/

Reproach yourself for every flaw/

Watch yourself go by every day/

Without taking the log out of your eyes/

try to see the speck in the eyes of others/

Stand by and watch yourself/

with a third eye/

If you'd do this/

It would dawn on you that you/

lack the moral high ground on/

which to stand and judge others/

Your love for others will grow like/

kokobioko[22] on a decaying tree/

In the same boat we all are/

The same fate awaits all men/

As one man is born, so is his brother/

As one man dies, so dies the other/

All of us breathe the same air/

The same red blood runs in our veins/

We defecate in the same way/

And urinate in like manner/

In coitus, we assume the same posture/

No man has an edge/

over another before our Creator/

Before God, all men are equal/

From dust we came, unto dust we shall return/

There are no greater or lesser beings/

We are all in the same boat/

Be you Francophone, Anglophone, or Non-phone!/

I call a spade a spade/

Couldn't care less whose ox is gored! /

That's because I am a scallywag/

I am a scallywag/

Take me or leave me/

That's your funeral!/

My chums are legion/

So are my foes/

I am a scallywag/

Love me or hate me/

I couldn't care less!/

I am humble/

But let not my humility/

be mistaken for cowardice/

I am a scallywag/

Berate me or extol me/

I don't give a hoot!/

I am who I am/

because I am who I am/

I am a scallywag/

I don't give a damn!/

This asteroid is screwed up!/

I wanna say what I gotta say/

No numskull's gonna/

Tell me to shut up!/

The underworld has put/

every dick in deep shit/

This gives me the creeps/

This joint's gone bunkers!/

Bunch of dirtballs have/

hijacked OUR Land! /

What do YOU make of that? /

So they're slaughtering/

in the name of tribalism? /

That's a load of crap! /

Thou shall not kill! /

Is the first law GIVEN to Adam and Eve/

Servants of Satan kill, Kill and Kill/

In the name of ethnocentrism/

PYRRHIC VICTORY!!! /

Kill! Kill! Kill! /

It's the spirit of the bayonet/

It's the lingo of the bullet/

Blood makes grass grow/

Blood! Blood! More blood! /

Victory starts here!

Methinks ours is but pyrrhic victory/

BRAVADO…

Bravado in futility…

You flex your muscles/

Your prime your gun/

You pull the trigger/

And fire fatal shots/

Poom! Poom! Poom!

Your foe drops dead/

in a pool of blood/

Does that solve the problem? /

Is there freedom in the casket? /

Is there License to kill? /

Humankind is deranged! /

Very sick, indeed/

I don't have to annihilate

in order to build/

That's the modus operandi

of bellicose nitwits/

Building castles in the air! /

I listen to the voice of reason/

in the haven of bellicosity/

crying out for peace/

I want to go the way of pacifism/

War-mongering being nothing

but bravado in futility/

These simpletons/

Are darned assholes/

Say they're a God-chosen tribe! /

Hard fact is they're frightened/

By the skeletons in their OWN closets/

Speak the truth and nothing but the truth/

Crusader…/

I am head and toes in a crusade/

The verses that you peruse NOW/

are my lethal ammunition/

against an ailing society/

A bazooka shoots to kill/

My pen scripts to annihilate/

Like a bulldozer it levels/

all minutiae in its path/

Graft, perversion, ineptitude/

corruption, tribalism/ nepotism, cronyism/

adultery, bigotry, racism, sexism/

gravy train and ilk/

A cannon booms to exterminate/

My pen writes to kill/

No one goes unscathed/

It has scores to settle/

with everyone and no one/

A missile detonates hitting/

every object in its orbit/

My pen blasts to lambaste butts/

right, left and center/

It's no respecter of social standing/

It doesn't revere social status/

I am the voice of the voiceless/

I am unfazed by all odds/

These verses that you read/

are an outburst of bitter emotions/

The pen is mightier than the sword!/

I am locked in mortal combat/

These lines over which you pore/

at this point in time/

are a figment of my imagination/

I am primed for the Vendetta/

against a venal society/

I tell it like it is/

Ere long, there'll be an onslaught! /

RAP ON THE VENAL…

Graft/

Tchoko[23]/

The bane of our nation/

Spoke in the wheel of nation-building/

I smell corruption everywhere/

I sniff nepotism all around/

I see it in all cracks and crevices/

Canker of the homeland/

Everywhere/

Favoritism reigns supreme/

Cronyism the national creed/

Mediocrity recompensed/

Virtuosity penalized/

What a load of hogwash! /

Le *père de la nation*[24] relishes kickbacks/

Le *planton*[25] wants *un petit quelque chose*[26]/

The *mbere khaki*[27] takes bribes/

The *zangalewa*[28] accepts gratification/

The *gendarme*[29] aids and abets corruption/

What a legacy for posterity! /

How long...

Shall we turn a blind eye/

to the crime and grime of our society? /

How long...

Shall we feign ignorance/

of the decadence that's eating/

deep into the moral fabric/

of our community? /

How long...

shall we not care a fig about/

the endemic poverty that/

has become our bedfellow? /

How long...

shall we not give a damn to/

the fact that our roads are death-tracks? /

How long...

shall we pretend not to see/

the siphoning of our natural resources/

by erstwhile colonial masters? /

How long…

shall we stay mute/

in the face of wanton abuse/

of the populace by belly-politicians? /

How long…

shall we overlook/

the fact that tribalism/

is our national leprosy? /

How long…

shall we make believe/

that when Yaoundé breathes/

la nation se porte bien[30]/

How long…

shall we delude ourselves/

that the end justifies the means? /

How long…

shall we continue/

to live in a neo-colonial fool's paradise? /

THE PARADISE OF IDIOTS

How long…

shall we continue/

to auction our nation/

to the highest bidder? /

How long…

shall we not see that/

Froggies and Anglos/

are wrapped in a bond/

of mutual distrust in *La République*?[31] /

How long…/

Smothering discontent/

may lurk around like the *nyamangoro*/ [32]

But there comes a time/

when even the *mbutuku*[33]/

picks up his boxing gloves/

like Mohammed Ali/

like ear-munching Mike Tyson/

And enters the ring/

to do battle with the foe/

till death do them part/

Rather than pick *tokyo*/ [34]

And run *nine-ninety*[35] like an *opep*/ [36]

hotly pursued by a *mange-mille*/[37]

So it came to pass in 1990/

When the *kanas*[38] man of Ntarikon/

Ni John Fru Ndi/

Our Latter Day Moses/

Bit the bullet and launched the/

Social Democratic Front (SDF)/

Amid much pomp and fanfare/

Political formation that's ere long been/

The albatross of Mbiya Mbivodo/

Absentee tenant at Etoudi/

Came fire/ came brimstone/

Came rain/came sun/

The aftermath was ravaging/

Numerous sons- of- the- soil/

And daughters- of- the- soil/

Cut down in their prime of youth/

Purportedly crushed in a stampede/

Myriads gave up the ghost in a bloodbath/

that left all and sundry dumfounded/

The truth of the matter is your guess/

As it's mine/

Several of my *tara*/[39]

picked up from *matango*[40] houses/

from matutu[41] taverns /

And from swine quarter/

thrown in ngata/[42].

None was a *sansanboy*/[43]

Sexually starved soldiers/

raped my *mini-minor*[44] sisters/

At Ngoa Ekelle/

Thousands more/

pounded like *poto-poto*/[45],

Lay rotting in mass graves_to date! /

Their ghosts ignited/

les villes mortes/

infamous ghost-town operations/

That brought economic life/

to a virtual standstill/

in Ongola/

Taximen and ba*yam-sellam*/[46]

Unsung heroes of No Man's Land /

Doggedly refused to throw in the towel/

The *Takembeng*/[47]

Symbol of feminine steel/

joined the processional dirge:

baying for Mbivodo's blood:

Barlok for youa head Mbivodo!/

Na helele-o!/

Trobu for youa pikin dem head Mbiya!/

Na heleie-o!/

Woman pawa na las pawa!/

Na helele-o! /

Tell we say no be woman born you! /

Na helele-o! /

Tell we say na mbouma born you/

Na helele-o! /

Bereaved families consulted/

maguida/[48] for *gris-gris*/[49]

Many more went to seek fortification/

from the *mami-wata*/[50]

The water gods of /

Lake Oku /

Lake Manenguba/

Sanaga River/

And Lake Nyos/

The intent?

Smoke Mbivodo/

And his Ali Baba Gang of thieves/

Out of the Shithouse at Etoudi /

Den of compulsive chop-broke-potters! /

hell-bent on crippling the nation/

via necromancy and megalomania/

through democraZy and kleptomania/

In Abakwa/

The downtrodden chanted:

Mbiya is really something!

He must go!

Facing Mount Cameroon/

Chariot of the gods/

The wretched of the earth roared/

Red card for Mbivodo!

In Bafoussam and Bafang/

In Loum Chantiers Gare/

In Penja and Dibombari/

In Nkongsamba and Kake/

In Mbanga and Penamboko/

Irate rioters sang freedoms songs: /

Liberté eh, eh! /

Liberté eh eh eh eh !/

Dieu tout puissant ah ah!/

Nous sommes libres bientôt!/

In Nkambe and Wainama/

In Bamunka and Babessi/

In Bamali and Babungo/

In Bambili and Bambui

In Bali and Babanki/

In Widikum and Wum/

Disillusioned protesters chorused: /

Liberty, eh, eh! /

Liberty eh, eh, eh, eh! /

All-powerful God, ah ah! /

Soon we'll be free! /

But the Man/

Being no spring chicken/

Smelling *arata*/[51] he sneaked incognito/

into the equatorial forest/

to obtain from his pygmy tribesmen/

megan[52] which he carried on his person

day in day out/

night and day/

as backup for his European-tailored/

bullet-proof jacket/

in his peregrinations/

across the ghost nation/

GHOST TOWNS OPERATIONS…

Towns haunted by ghosts of victims/

The ghost of Eric Takou/

Phantoms of freedom fighters/

cut down by bullets fired by/

trigger-happy soldiers and *gendarmes*/[53]

haunt the land in perpetuity/

The brutal killing of innocent kids/

shocked women who exposed their vaginas/

to the killers protesting/

the murder of innocent kids/

The corpse of Takou/

Paraded in a *pousse-pousse*[54]/

by incensed inhabitants of Douala/

found its way to the doorstep of his assassin/

VENDETTA…

First it had been students/

Then came civil servants/

Now the black marketers

joined the macabre dance/

Refusing to be subdued/

by municipal vampires/

They stood firm in the face of imminent danger/

Then came the turn of taxi drivers/

Who refused to commute/

Protesting the legal shakedowns by the police/

They mourned colleagues/

shot at point-blank range/

by *mbere khaki*[55] /

then came the turn of *bendskin*[56] drivers/

who took to the streets of New Bell/

to protest the brutal killing of one/

of theirs murdered by a *mange-mille* on duty/

The deceased had refused to *tchoko*[57]/

Commuters had gone on strike/

to protest this endemic human cruelty/

The day they went on strike/

all streets were emptied of its human cargo/

From time to time/

A helicopter would cross the sky/

Men ducked and dived in *boutiques*[58]

And off-license bars/

Purporting that the helicopter carried tear-gas/

And machine-guns/

Grenades/and bombs!

In that fateful year/

the *têtes brulées*[59] man of Nooremac,

stuck out their necks in defiance/

of the junta in Yaoundé/

Resistance is defiance/

Amidst elephantine opposition/

masterminded by the Beti-led/

pseudo-government in Ongola/

the people stood firm/

Resistance is defiance/

The aftermath of the heroic venture/

was macabre and sinister/

All kept a stiff upper lip/

Resistance is defiance/

Many more sodomized and brutalized/

by gun-totting lunatics/

in military fatigues/

Many hundreds ended up in the infamous BMM—/

Brigade Mixte Mobile up-station/

Bamenda pikin chopped fire[60]/

in the face of tyranny/

Resistance is defiance/

Weep not BRETHREN! /

We'll overcome! /

Your sweat did not ooze in vain/

Now, some brad you 'sell-outs'/

Others say you've eaten soya[61]/

Many claim you've dined/

with the Gaullist Mammon/

Give them the lie! /

Friends and foes may croak/

Le chien aboie et la caravane passe[62] /

Resistance is defiance/

Falter not brothers! /

Freedom shall be ours/

We shall overcome/

Come rain come thunder! /

The liberation of your brethren/

West of the Mungo River/

shall be the ultimate victory/

Fear not sisters! /

Cowards die many times/

before their real death/

Resistance is defiance/

The permutation of Events/

Put the center on the periphery/

And the periphery in the center/

The center is no longer the center/

When things fall apart[63] /

The centripetal forces of nationhood/

Disintegrate alongside centrifugal forces/

Uninterrupted processes of decentralization/

And disunity in full gear/

Pandora's Box…

The contradiction-filled/

Tension-filled unity of post-colonial Kamerun/

Bogged down in corporeal trivia/

At the expense of cognitive self-cultivation/

Il faut cultiver son jardin[64]/

The cross-pollination of ideas/

Being life's tonic/

Unity is strength…

SUMUNYE….

Simunye!

We're one!

Many tribes/ many tongues/

Bakossi, Bakundu, Bekwere…

Nations within a Nation/

Simunye!

We're one!

Many peoples/one Destiny

Graffi/Nkwa/Fulani/Bororo

Simunye!

We're one!

From the grassfields of Bamenda/

To the coastal lands of the Littoral

Sprouts a New Nation/

The Rainbow Nation /

Sing Simunye!

We're one!

Toyi! Toyi![65]

War song of the downtrodden/

Dirge of martyrdom/

Takes two to tango/

And a throng to *toyi-toyi*.

Sing *toyi! toyi!*

To the fallen heroes/

of Ntarikon Park/

Sing *toyi! toyi!*

To the unsung heroines/

of Lake Nyos/

Chant *toyi! toyi!*

To the demise of segregation/

And to the death/

of *Francofolie*[66] /

Chorus toyi*! toyi!*

To the assassins/

of *Anglofolie*[67] /

Justice delayed/

is justice denied.

Sing *toyi! toyi!*

SING UBUNTU…

Ubuntu…

In my native land/

We don't wear masks! /

Camaraderie being second nature/

In my homeland/

Anyone's everyone's keeper/

We don't erect invisible fences/

We live in unison/

In my fatherland selfless service/

is the modus vivendi/

Egoism being extraneous/

to our way of life/

In my native village/

self-effacement is/

the unwritten law/

vanity being anathema/

to our very being/

In my culture/

We live a communal life/

That's why we sing UBUNTU/

Sing H-u-r-u-j-e!

H-u-r-u-j-e! of national reconstruction…/

H-u-r-u-j-e of *Hunchbackers*[68]/

Sing H-u-r-u-j-e!!! /

Time to re-possess the *hunchback*![69]/

H-u-r-u-j-e! /

Dawn of a UNITED NOOREMAC???

Or dusk of the crippled offspring of Foumban??? /

H-u-r-u-j-e!/

Sons and daughters of Donga Mantung/

H-u-r-u-j-e!/

Men and women of Kousseri/

H-u-r-u-j-e!/

The foot soldiers of national reconciliation /

H-u-r-u-j-e!/

Boys and girls of Kupe Manenguba/

H-u-r-u-j-e!/

Warriors against neo-pessimism/

H-u-r-u-j-e!/

Combatants against battered self-image/

H-u-r-u-j-e!/

Commanders of NOOREMAC's Salvation Army/

H-u-r-u-j-e!

NOOREMAC must unite or perish /

H-u-r-u-j-e!/

It boggles the mind /

To think that we will/

salvage this Nation by/

balkanizing it into ethnic concaves/

into tribal fiefs and war zones/

This sort of tinkering spells doom/

The future of NOOREMAC/

rests on our collective wisdom/

We cannot but unite/

Behind one banner/

to address the collective mishaps/

that have befallen us/

Welcome a-board!

Gird your loins/

Sing Kum-Kum Massa!

Oh! Kum-Kum!

H-u-r-u-j-e!

Kamerunian youths/

Oh! Kum-Kum!

The turn is yours/

Oh! Kum-Kum!

H-u-r-u-j-e!

Kamerunian women/

Oh! Kum-Kum!

Big, big *ngondere*[70]/

Oh! Kum-Kum!

Small, small *ngondere*[71]/

Oh! Kum-Kum!

All hands on deck/

Oh! Kum-Kum!

One time! GO! NOOREMAC! /

GO NOOREMAC! /GO!

Pick up the flickering torch/

NO TURNING BACK!

United we stand/

Divided we fall/

The onus is ours/

To rescue NOOREMAC/

Rescue NOOREMAC

from re-colonization/

from neo-colonization/

NOOREMAC …

Not a country for the taking/

Not the lost country/

Not a free-for-all/

NOOREMAC …

Not the bread basket of the Gaulles/

Not a country at risk/

NOOREMAC …

Not a tabula rasa/

Not a clean slate/

NOOREMAC ...

Has not reached/

The proverbial point-

Of-no-return /

NOOREMAC ...

Is not unredeemable/

Neo-pessimists/

Despoilers of our backyard/

May say what they like/

They're like termites...

These insects don't build/

They destroy/

Crogg/ Crogg/ Crogg/

They've destroyed our economies/

They've destroyed our coffee plants/

TERMITES...

These insects don't nurture/

They devastate/

They've destroyed our industries/

Produce Marketing Board/

Sonara Limbe/

Ndu Tea/

Tole Tea/

Socapalm/

Cameroon Development Corporation/

Cameroon Bank/

Mideno and Midevif/

Upper Nun Valley Development Authority/

Cragg/ Cragg/ Caogg/

They are termites/

They've destroyed our livelihood/

They've destroyed our palm trees/

They've destroyed our rubber trees/

They don't save; they annihilate/

They've destroyed our banana plantations/

They've destroyed our plantain plantations/

They don't plant they reap/

Where they didn't sow/

They've depleted our forests/

They've destroyed the source of our income/

Crugg/ Crugg/ Crugg/

Termites…

These insects are hard at work/

Destroying the legacy/

Bequeathed to us by our forebears/

Termites are in charge of our collective destiny...

Steer clear of the *makanana*[72] town criers/

They are termites/

Shall they make or mar? /

That is the question/

It's time for an extirpation of conscience/

They're KLEPTOMANIACS!

Kleptomania…

Rigor and moralization/

Go ahead, Mbiya! /

Go ahead Father of the Nation/

We are behind you/

Go ahead National Guide/

We support your every action/

With faith and unity/

Rigor and moralization/

Eat your share Mbiya/

The trough is full/

Just eat your share/

Grave-digger of the Nation/

Eat your share with rigor and immorality/

We support your inaction/

Of infidelity and off-handedness/

Eat your part with rigor and infatuation/

Eat your share and leave us alone/

Assume the task Mbiya/

Father of the ghost-nation/

Eat your share Mbiya/

Always sexy guy/

Do not relent in your mission of dilapidation/

With rigor and determination/

You are God's gift to us/

Pursue your mission/

We are behind you/

What can we do? /

We're undone/

Down with doomsayers! /

Down with kleptomaniacs!

Long live rigor and moralization! /

They're WITCHES/

Witchcraft…

Concocted in heathen laboratories/

you passed off as indigenous science/

Yet you are the bane of humanity/

Your macabre deeds legion/

permeating all the nooks/

and crannies of the globe/

People call you *juju*/

Some call you *famla*/

Others brand you *magan*/

Many christen you *tobassi*/

I call you *gris-gris*

My significant other brands/

you *mbungo chobi*

What's in a name? /

Truth of the matter? /

You are our arch-enemy! /

In your name/

Families are torn asunder/

In your name/

The elderly kill the young/

In your name/

The young brutalize the old/

In your name/

Houses are torched at random/

In your name/

Kangaroo courts judge the innocent/

In your name/

The law is flouted with impunity/

Through your diabolical forces/

Inept leaders stay in power/

In perpetuity/

Witchcraft…

You set parents against offspring/

Through you/

The evil-minded wreak havoc/

Sibling rises against sibling/

You pit friend against friend/

Witchcraft…

You're a stumbling to social harmony/

It's high time we bade you farewell/

ADIEU…

Thank Goodness! /

Thank heavens! /

At long last I've this inferno/

Behind me for good/

The Jungle Republic/

Wherein Man is Man's worst enemy/

Thank Goodness!

At the end of the day/

I'm out of this Ali Baba den/

Where Humanity is fodder for humanity/

Thank God! /

Finally, I can now pack/

Bag and baggage/

And say adieu to these vampires/

I leave behind a human Zoo/

In which some animals/

Are worthier than others/

Dieu merci![73]

I can now shake the dust/

off my blistered feet/

And say farewell to the Bastion/

of tomfoolery and *feymania*[74]/

Thank Heavens! /

I am on the run again/

I leave this land/

Without regrets/

Firm in my conviction that/

Old habits die hard/

Hard to teach an old monkey new tricks/

When all is said and done/

Nooremac remains in the throes/

Of developmental inertia/

It's hell on earth!

Where the rich feed feces to the poor/

Ruben Um Nyobé might have given up the ghost/

For the sake of Nooremacans/

Ernest Ouandié might have been/

Eliminated on January 16, 1971/

In the name of Nooremac/

Bishop Albert Ndongmo might have/

Been arrested and convicted/

In December 1970/

In the name of Nooremacans/

Wambo le Courant/

Might have been a "partner in crime"

With Albert Ndongmo/

For the sake of Nooremac/

Félix-Roland Moumié/

Nooremac's Marxist leader/

Might have been eliminated/

In Geneva by the SDECE/

(French Secret service) with thalium/

Ndeh Ntumazah and Albert Womah Mukong/

Might have put their lives/

In jeopardy in the name of Nooremacans/

Alas, the wheel of national/

Disintegration continues to grind/

And grind, and grind, and grind/

Thanks Goodness! /

I am leaving this slaughterhouse/

Where governance is by the corrupt/

of the corrupt, and for the corrupt/

Thank God I am leaving/

In one piece and not in pieces/

I go in peace to where/

there are no human rights violations/

I go in peace to where/

there is no discrimination/

between language groups and ethnic groups/
I go in peace to where/

there is no overt dictatorship/

When a people don't know/

Where they're going/

Maybe that's because/

They don't know/

where they're coming from/

And if they don't know/

where they come from/

Maybe that's because/

they don't know their own history/

Oftentimes/ we've been branded/

the lost generation of Ngola/

Some have christened/

the children if this land *fufu*/[75] for military canon/

Maybe that's because/

the future holds no good/

for the *jeune tale*nt/[76] of this blighted nation/

caught in the crossfire/ of political *djintété*[77]/

When the *grand katika*[78] fight/

The *tchotchoro*[79] of Ngola/

leak their gaping wounds/

Smouthering discontent/

may crawl like the *nyamangoro*/[80]

But there comes a time/ when even the *mbut*[81]/

Picks up his boxing gloves/

And enters the ring/

Rather than pick *tokio*/[82]

And run *nine-ninety*[83] like an *opep*/[84]

being hotly pursued by a *mange-mille*/[85]

So it came to pass in 1990/

When the *kanas*[86] man/ of Ntarikon/

Ni John Fru Ndi/

Bit the bullet/ and launched/

the Social Democratic Front/

Political formation/ that's ere long been/

The albatross of Mr. Mbiya./

current tenant at Etoudi/

Came fire/ came brimestone/

Came rain/came sun/

The aftermath ravaging/

Numerous youngsters/ cut down in the/

Prime of their youth/

Zillions lost their lives/

Purportedly crushed in a stampede/

The truth of the matter/ is everyone's guess/

Several of my *tara*/[87]

were picked up from *matango*[88] houses/

and thrown in ngata/[89].

None was a *sansanboy*/[90]

Sexually starved soldiers/

raped my *mini-minor*[91] sisters/

At Ngoa Ekelle/Thousands more/

pounded/ like *poto-poto*/[92],

Lie rotting/ in mass graves to date!/

Their ghosts/ ignited/

the infamous ghost-town operations/

That brought the economic life of Ngola/ to a standstill/

Taximen and ba*yam-sellam*/[93] refused to throw in the towel/

The *Takembeng*/[94] joined the dirge/

baying for Mbiya's blood/

Bereaved families/ consulted *maguida*/[95] for *gris-gris*/[96]

Many more/ went to seek help/ from the *mami-wata*[97]

In Lake Oku /and Lake Nyos/ to no avail.

The intent/ smoke Mbiya/

out of his hide-out/ at the Etoudi Presidential palace/

In Bamenda/ rioters chanted:

"Mbiya is really something!

He must go,

Red card for Mbiya!"

In Bafoussam/ people sang:

Liberté eh, eh/

Liberté eh eh eh eh/

Dieu tout puissant ah ah!/

Nous sommes libres bientôt!/

In Buea protesters chorused:

Liberty, eh, eh/

Liberty eh, eh, eh, eh!/

All-powerful God, ah ah!/

Soon we'll be free!/

But the man/ no spring kitchen/

Smelling *arata*/[98] he sneaked into

The equatorial forest/

to obtain from his pygmy tribesmen/

megan[99] /carried on him/ day in day out /

backup to his bullet-proof jacket/

GHOST TOWNS

Towns haunted/by ghosts of victims/

The ghost of Eric Takou/ haunts in Douala/

The brutal killing/ of the innocent kid/

Shocked all and sundry/

the corpse of Takou /paraded in a wheel-barrow /

by insensed inhabitants of Douala/ was later/

deposited at the home of his murderer/

TAXI MEN

First it had been the students/

Then some civil servants/

Now the black marketers/ got into the dance/

Refusing to be eaten alive/ by municipal vampires/

Then came the turn of taxi drivers/

Who refused to commute/ to protest/

the legal shakedowns by the police/

they mourned a taxi driver/

shot at point-blank range/

by a mbere khaki/

to whom he had refused to tchoko[100]/

taximen had gone on strike/

to protest this endemic human cruelty/

The day they went on strike/ all streets were empty/

From time to time/ a helicopter crossed the sky/

Men hid in shops and *matango*[101] houses/

Purporting the helicopter carried tear gas/

And machine guns/

Harbinger of the arrival of Mermaids—

FALLEN HEROES

Hail Bate Besong!

Hail Bole Butake!

Hail Bernard Nsokkika Fonlon!

Hail Sam Novala Fonkem!

Hail Albert Womah Mukong!

Hail Ndeh Tumazah!

There aren't here/

Yet far and away/

Echoes of their prolific

Erudition resounds/

BB's not here/

But the legacy of his

intellect lives here/

He's not here/

but rumblings of his

vociferous castigation

of an inept system clamors/

He's is not here/

still far and wide

the melody of his vociferation

against a cancerous polity chimes/

Hail Obasinjom Warrior!

The genuine intellectual/

The man who relegated

phony intellectualism

to the trashcan of academe/

Bate Besong is no more

Long live Bate Besong !

Long live the immortal!

Big or small/

Rich or poor/

Corruptible or incorruptible/

Miscreant or holier-than-thou/

From dust you came/

Unto dust you'll return.

Hail Reuben Um Nyobé!

bête noire of the Gaulois and of Ahmadou Ahidjo/

Maquisard/ of the Sanaga Maritime forest/

Die-hard upecist/

He wandered in the heart of dark forests/

Feeding on roots and branches/

Oblivious to birds of ill-omen/

He wandered on the banks of the River Sanaga/

Eating raw fish and roasted cassava/

He wandered in the deep of night/

Tiptoeing in and out of his hideouts/

He wandered in the burning bushes/

Alert to sounds of birds of good-omen/

And they offered him good tidings…

BAOBAB…

He was a Lion-man/

A man with a heart of steel /

A Man with the tongue of fire

A Man born before his age/

He knew the nooks and crannies of

Conspiratorial machinations—

the ultimate declaration of love-hate

for the arch-enemy/

UNSUNG HERO

Albert Womah Mukong

Pet-peeve of Ahidjoic inept regime/

Recidivist inmate/ prisoner without a crime/

of Mantoun concentration camp/

Graduate of Nkondengui/

maximum security dungeon/

Hail Ernest Ouandié!

Object of public opprobrium/

sacrificial lamb/ of political thuggery/

Chagrin of the Upecist/ashes of freedom/

Flesh of flesh/bone of bone

But the iroko tree refused to lend him/

a hand in the struggle/

but the mahogany tree refused/

 to embrace him in the combat

but the baobab trees refused him their shade/

in the Sanaga swamps /

the equatorial jungle was closed to

his quest for shelter/ it was said to him/

the revolution has been made without him/

his tribesmen disowned him/

to the utter dismay of the groaning hyenas.

Is there a crisis of identity?

IDENTITY CRISIS

I don't quite know/ who I am/

Je ne sais/ pas au juste/ qui je suis.

Some call me/ Anglo/

D'autres m'appellent/ Frog/

I still don't know/ who I am/

Je ne sais toujours pas/ qui je suis/

My name/ c'est /Le Bamenda/

My name/ is /L'Ennemi dans la maison/

My name/ c'est/ le Biafrais/

Mon nom/ is/ underclass citizen/

My name/ c'est/ le maladroit/

Taisez-vous! /Shut up!/

Don't bother me!/

Ne m'embêtez pas!/

Don't you know/ that /je suis ici chez moi?/

Vous ignorez /que/ I belong here?/

I shall fight/ to my dernier souffle/

to forge/ a real name/ pour moi-même/

You/ shall call me/ Anglofrog!/

Vous/ m'appelerez/ Franglo!/

Shut up! Taisez-vous!/

Don't bother me!/

Ne m'embêtez pas!/

Vous ignorez/ que/ I belong here?/

Don't you know/ that/ je suis ici chez moi?/

I shall fight/ to my last breath/

to forge/ a real lingo/ for myself/

I'll speak Français/

Je parlerai English/

Together/ we'll speak camfranglais/

C'est-à-dire/ qu'ensemble/

We'll speak/ le Camerounisme/

Because/ ici nous sommes tous/ chez nous/

A bon entendeur/ salut!/

He who has ears/ should hear!

Hear the macabre dance

BREAK-DANCE…

IN NGOLA

Tchoum/Tchoum

Ntarikonic requiem of zombification/

Tchoumassa of disembowelers/

Tchoumassa /of defilers of girls in their teens/

Of despoilers /of teenagers in the taxi-cab/

And of grave-diggers at Nkoulouloun/

Of beheaders of schoolkids at Mokolo/

Tchoum/Tchoum

Tchoumassa of vampires/

One/ two/three/four

Stamp your club-feet/

Grab your partner/ mami wata/ by the waist/

Turn her around to fact the heath fire/

Tchoum/Tchoum/Tchoumassa

This is the credo of *alikamouti*[102]/

consumer of hot flesh/ regurgitating/

the entrails/the meat

of victims of poisoned gifts/

Tchoum/Tchoum

Tchoumassa/

Credo/ of men the underworld/

Of *coupeur de rou*te/ the high-way robber/

Hunted by forces of law and order/

In love with *Dan sapak*[103]/

WOLOWOSS[104]

GALORE…

Looking at these images/

Your gait/ your demeanor/speaks volumes/

So robbed of your self/

Young girl / mini-skirter/ere long deflowered/

Young woman/ with revealing dress/man hunter/

That tells tales about your lot in life/

Heart-broken I am/looking at these images

OF YOU AND OF ILK

And you *sit*a[105]/obligated to

Trade your soul for a penny/

And for a living you're thingified/

nothing more to say…

AND YOU

Scavenger of public scum/

Hands sullied with social grime/

crime of tribalism/of cronyism/of nepotism…

trio opium/ nationwide

AND YOU

Prison graduate/ in cell number zero/

prisoner without a crime/Cruxified on the cross/

of witch-hunt

THE POET

To write or not to write/

Fornicator of ideas/ pulverizer of illusions/

Self-delusion/canker/ demise of a nation unborn/

ME

I write poetry/Therefor I am/

Harbinger of ill-wind/

To speak or not to speak/

THE BARD

Voice of the voiceless/

Quiet peace-lover/ loquacious/

Taciturn talkative

YOU…

Scavenger of social scum/

You create your own world/

A wordl of toxication/

YOU… ME…TOWN CRIER

We create worlds of PREVARICATION

Man and man are locked

 in infectious suspicion/

Wife thinks husband is lying.

Husband believes wife is lying/

Child thinks parent is lying/

Parent thinks child is lying/

The tax-collector

thinks the taxpayer is lying/

The taxpayer believes

the tax-collector is lying.

The politician thinks

the electorate is lying/

Voters think the

Candidates are lying/

 Pretty load of hogwash!

Garbed in multifaceted masks/

They make believe in all walks of life/

Foes act like friends/

Friends ape foes/

Mortals impersonate immortals/

Humans pass for super-humans/

Miscreants act the pious/

Self-seekers masquerade/

as selfless philanthropists/

The Muses said this would happen:

That language/ would be hijacked/

And words twisted/

By a couple of tricksters/

From the Department of Double-Speak/

SLANGUAGE…

Penchant for convoluted lingo/

Notoriety to make the ordinary/

Look extraordinary/

Influence peddling has become

Scratch my back I scratch your own!

Corruption and theft from government

Has become *la chèvre broute la où*

Elle est attachée!

Homosexuality has been rebaptised as Pédé!

Unlicensed driving is now called clando!

Et patati patata.

Auto mechanics have become

Automobile internists/

Elevator operators pass for

vertical transportation corps/

Double-speak/ your stock-in-trade/

Pre-emptive counter-attack

Veils your compulsive belligerence/

Tactical redeployment/

is the euphemism for military retreat/

The Vietnam War dubbed

You no longer talk

about bullet holes/

They're ballistically induced apertures/

In the subcutaneous environment/

Our neutron bombs/

Have metamorphosed into/

Radiation enhancement contraption/

Double-speak breeds fire-power/

I can barely comprehend/

What I desire/

I speak words/

That I do not know/

Where they're going/

We're in the wilderness now/

Confused by signs/

We're in the fast train/

Where we need stop lights/

To halt the insanity/

We're in the top-speed metro/

Where we need red lights/

To stop the indulgence/

We're in the breakneck train

Where are need traffic lights/

To halt the dementia/

We're in the maddening train/

where we need stop lights/

to put an end to madness.

We're in the high-speed train

where we need yellow lights/

to halt the derangement/

And from then on/

Words have gotten crooked/

And more and more crooked/

Until no one would understand/

What the other is saying/

Or to look at the mouth/

Of his neighbor/

When it is best to shut up/

And sing Kumkum Massa.

Huruje! Huruje! Huruje!

Kunkum Massa! Oh !

Kunkum Massa!Oh!

Huruje! Huruje! Huruje!

African youth/

The turn is yours!

Huruje! Huruje! Huruje!

Kunkum Massa! Oh !

Kunkum Massa!Oh!

African women/

Big, big ngondere!

Small, small ngondere

Huruje! Huruje! Huruje!

Kunkum Massa! Oh !

Kunkum Massa!Oh!

Hands on deck!

Huruje! Huruje! Huruje!

Kunkum Massa! Oh !

Kunkum Massa!Oh!

Huruje! Huruje! Huruje!

One time! GO! GO!GO!

Pick up the flickering torch

of African UNITY.

The onus is yours.

We live in troubled times/

That they had predicted/

Nothing means what it says/

And our words say what was not meant.

Notes

1 There is no way out.

2 Joe La Conscience, whose real name is Kameni Joe de Vinci, is a Cameroonian musician who organized a one-man nonviolent protest against President Paul Biya's attempt to amend article 6.2 of the Cameroonian constitution in 2008.Joe wrote a memorandum tilted "50 Good reasons to not change the constitution' to protest against plans to scrap the presidential terms limits that would make the incumbent president for life. He also composed a song condemning the planned constitutional amendment titled "Emmerdement constitutionnel (Constitutional hassle).Consequently, he was arrested by security forces and jailed at the Maximum security prison at Kondengui in Yaoundé. The next day, troops stormed his residence in Loum and shot his 11-year-old son, Aya Kameni Patrick Lionnel to death.

3 Lapiro de Mbanga alias Ndinga Man (= Guitar Man). Born in Mbanga as Pierre Roger Sandjo Lambo, Lapiro de Mbanga is a songwriter known for his satiric lyrics, criticizing politicians and addressing social and economic injustice in Cameroon, Singing mainly in Pidgin English, Cameroonian Creole, he is able to reach a broad audience in all strata of society, especially those where his diatribes are well received, i.e., the young urban unemployed, cart-pushers, hawkers, *sauveteurs*, street sellers, *beyam sellam*, taxi and *bendskin* drivers. Lapiro has earned the nickname *Président du petit peuple* or "President of the struggling people" on account of his committed music. He too was arrested and jailed at the same time with Joe La Conscience.

4 President of street hawkers

5 The writ of Habeas Corpus has historically been an important instrument for the safeguarding of individual freedom against arbitrary state action.

6 Latin phrase that translates into English as "my fault", or "my own fault".

7 And so on and so forth

8 Cameroon Peoples' Demagogic Party (C.P.D.M), pejorative term coined by this poet to describe the demagogues at the helm of the party in power in Cameroon.

[9] Term used derogatorily by Francophone Cameroonians in reference to their Anglophone compatriots.

[10] Biafrans. This term is generally used by Francophone Cameroonians in reference to Anglophone Cameroonians whom they consider "outsiders" in Cameroon.

[11] Insulting epithet used by Francophone Cameroonians in reference to people from the North West Province of Cameroon.

[12] Quote from George Orwell's *Animal Farm* (1946)

[13] The epidemic that is decimating Cameroonians East and West of the Mungo River.

[14] Longuè Longuè whose real name is Longkana Agno Simon is a committed Cameroonian musician whose musical albums, namely *Ayo Africa*(2001), *Privatisation* (2003) and *Le libérateur libéré* (2006) have endeared him to the suffering masses.

[15] The belief in living a hand to mouth life; and not saving for the future.

[16] Country

[17] Student who has passed the Baccalauréat, the equivalent of the General Certificate of Education (G.C.E) Advanced Level.

[18] Holder of a bachelor's degree.

[19] French equivalent of the Anglo-Saxon PhD

[20] A metaphor for professors who climb up the ranks not through scholarship and merit, but through gossip, slander and "toeing the line" of the university administration and the regime in power(cf.Dibussi and Ashutantang(2008), p.58).

[21]Scholars with little or no academic pedigree who are not interested in scholarship and critical thinking (cf.Dibussi and Ashutantang, op. cit., p.57).

[22] Mushrooms

[23] Small bribe

[24] Head of state

[25] Office messenger

[26] Small bribe

[27] Policeman

[28] Soldier

[29] Police in francophone African countries

[30] The nation is faring well.

[31] The republic.

[32] Literally "snail"; by extension, both a slow, nonchalant person and trivial affair.

[33] Abbreviated from the word "mbutuku", which means "a good-for-nothing person, "a weakling," or "an idiot". Mainly used by young people, this loanword exists in Cameroon Pidgin English since the 1970s.

[34] Run

[35] Fast

[36] Illegally operated taxi.

[37] The lowest ranking member of the police force, unbeatable when it comes to extorting taxi drivers on the streets. Literally, it means "eat-a-thousand"

[38] Male genitals, testicles; courage

[39] Friends

[40] Palm-wine

[41] Raffia wine

[42] Prison

[43] Smart boy, rascal

[44] Refers to a young woman who has not yet attained puberty. In some contexts it may refer to a young prostitute.

[45] Mud; valueless. The presence of this word in Cameroonian French dates from the 1940s.

[46] Market women.

[47] Group of post-menopausal women participating in a protest.

[48] Muslim from the north of Cameroon

[49] Amulets

[50] Water spirits who, from time to time, come to torment men.

[51] Rat

[52] Witchcraft

[53] Police officer in francophone Africa

[54] Wheel-cart

[55] Policemen

[56] Motor-bike taxi drivers.

[57] Give a bribe.

[58] Shops.

[59] Courageous people.

[60] Children of Bamenda refused to budge.

[61] Others say you have struck a deal with the enemy.

[62] The dog barks as the caravan goes by.

[63] Reference to Chinua Achebe's classic novel *Things Fall Apart*, 1958

[64] We must cultivate our minds.

[65] Protest march in South Africa in the era of Apartheid.

[66] The inanity of Francophones.

[67] The erratic behavior of Anglophones.

[68] Anglophone Cameroonians (see Dibussi and Ashutantang, op.cit. p.56).

[69] Refers to that part of the map of Cameroon which protrudes like a hunchback and which corresponds to the former British Southern Cameroons or Anglophone Cameroon. (See Dibussi and Ashutantang, op.cit. p.56).

[70] Mature women

[71] Teenage girls

[72] Language of the Beti tribe.

[73] Thank God.

[74] The evil deeds of conmen.

[75] Also spelt foufou and fou-fou; dough made from corn. Fufu is one of the staple dishes of Cameroonians from the Northwest Province.

[76] Young children

[77] Bigshot

[78] From the English word "care-taker". The word refers to a security guard in charge of a public place like a cinema , recreation ground, casino, etc. it entered Cameroon Pidgin English in the late 1980s among urban dwellers, as expressed essentially in oral discourse.

[79] Little children. Speakers of Cameroon Pidgin English have used this word since 1980s.

[80] Literally "snail"; by extension, both a slow, nonchalant person and trivial affair.

[81] Abbreviated from the word " mbutuku", which means " a good-for-nothing person, " a weakling" or "an idiot". Many used by young people, this loanword exists in Cameroon Pidgin English since the 1970s.

[82] Run

[83] Fast

[84] Illegally operated taxi.

[85] The lowest ranking member of the police force, unbeatable when it comes to extorting taxi drivers on the streets. Literally, it means " eat-a-thousand".

[86] Male genitals, testicles; courage

[87] Friends

[88] palm-wine

[89] Prison

[90] Smart boy, rascal

[91] Refers to a young woman who has not yet attained puberty. In some contexts it may refer to a young prostitute.

[92] Mud, valueless. The presence of this word in Cameroonian French dates from the 1940s.

[93] Market women.

[94] Group of elderly women

[95] Muslim from the north of Cameroon

[96] Amulets

[97] Female water spirits who, from time to time come to torment men.

[98] Rat

[99] Witchcraft

[100] give a bribe

[101] palm-wine

[102] vampire

[103] prostitute

[104] prostitute

[105] sister

Printed in the United States
by Baker & Taylor Publisher Services